Effective Publicity Using Media

By

David K. Ewen, M.Ed.

www.ForestAcademy.org

Copyright © 2013, Ewen Prime Company, Inc.
All rights reserved

ISBN-13: 978-1492792529
ISBN-10: 1492792527

Effective Publicity Using Media

David K. Ewen, M.Ed.

Forest Academy

Topics

- Difference between marketing and publicity
- Marketing formula and strategy
- Publicity resources and media communication

Difference between Marketing & Publicity

The difference between marketing and publicity is the following:

Marketing is what is said or written to the customer or client

Publicity is the delivery of the marketing content.

Sales is Marketing plus Publicity. Sales is Marketing planning first followed by Publicity.

An example is the ad in a newspaper is marketing. The delivery of the newspaper to the community is publicity. The buying action of a customer or client resulting from the ad in the newspaper is Sales.

This course talks about both marketing and publicity. A marketing expert with clients consisting of fortune 500 companies was in agreement that many organizations fail in sales goals because they do not know how to sell. The reason is that they meld marketing and publicity together for their sales efforts rather than focusing first on marketing and then the publicity. By splitting up the big beast of Sales into smaller pieces of Marketing and Publicity, it is easier to focus on the mission, goal, and objective of each. The individual completion of planning of Marketing followed by Publicity makes for an effective Sales plan.

Marketing

Marketing

This is the formula to represent yourself. It's easy to explain, but very hard to do.

- WIIFM = (It/This) will (Make/Give) you __(why?/passion)__
- RASCIL = Reliability, Authenticity, Simplicity, Completeness, Illustration, Location
- 5 W's = Who, What, When, Where, Why

Together, they have a combined formula / Copyright (c) 2012, David K. Ewen, M.Ed.

Who
What ├──── Who & What = RASCIL
When .... Time frame
Where .... Location
Why = WIIFM

Copyright (c) 2012, David K. Ewen, M.Ed.

WIIFM is What's In It For Me

WIIFM = (It/This) will (Make/Give) you __(why?/passion)__

Some examples are:

- It will make you happy
- This will make you successful
- It will give you chills
- This will give you love

WIIFM represents the

- Passion
- Why
- Result
- Impact

WIIFM - Common Mistakes

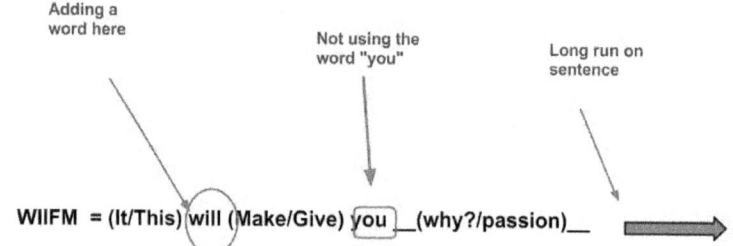

WIIFM - Intent of Formula

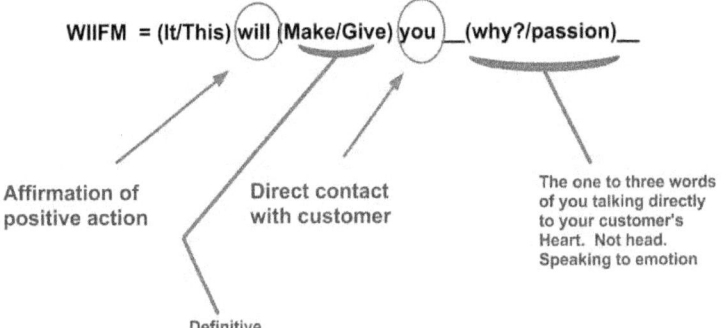

WIIFM = (It/This) will (Make/Give) you __(why?/passion)__

- Affirmation of positive action
- Definitive
- Direct contact with customer
- The one to three words of you talking directly to your customer's Heart. Not head. Speaking to emotion

Example: WIIFM

Scary Book from Stephen King

WIIFM = (It/This) will (Make/Give) you __ Emotion / Impact __

- This will make you scream
- It will give you chills
- This will give you nightmares
- It will make you shiver

11 ~ www.ForestAcademy.org ~ 11

RASCIL represent the WHO & WHAT. It is to be used as a general guide to help ensure facts aren't missed.

The origin of RASCIL is the design of yellow page ads

- R = Reliability   Length of service / longevity
- A = Authenticity   Certificates, licenses, degrees, accolades, testimonies, reviews
- S = Simplicity   Easy access to your product or service
- C = Completeness Different lines of business & channels of customers
- I = Illustration   Logo or overall look
- L = Location   How are you contacted? Address? Phone? Email? Website?

Use an example of a family owned auto mechanic garage in the yellow pages.

- R = Reliability   ... Since 1976
- A = Authenticity   ... ACE Certified
- S = Simplicity   ... Early drop off, weekend hours
- C = Completeness ... Oil change, mufflers, auto body repair, tires
- I = Illustration   ... Picture of clean garage with tools hanging neatly
- L = Location   ... Address, phone

RASCIL

RASCIL represent the WHO & WHAT. It is to be used as a general guide to help ensure facts aren't missed.

The origin of RASCIL is the design of yellow page ads

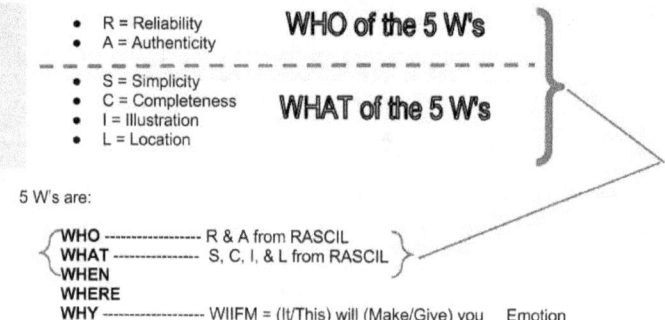

- R = Reliability
- A = Authenticity

WHO of the 5 W's

- S = Simplicity
- C = Completeness
- I = Illustration
- L = Location

WHAT of the 5 W's

5 W's are:

- WHO ----------- R & A from RASCIL
- WHAT ---------- S, C, I, & L from RASCIL
- WHEN
- WHERE
- WHY ----------- WIIFM = (It/This) will (Make/Give) you __Emotion__

~ www.ForestAcademy.org ~

RASCIL

RASCIL represent the **WHO & WHAT**. It is to be used as a general guide to help ensure facts aren't missed.

The origin of RASCIL is the design of yellow page ads

- R = Reliability — Length of service / longevity
- **→** A = Authenticity — Certificates, licenses, degrees, accolades, testimonies, reviews
- S = Simplicity — Easy access to your product or service
- C = Completeness — Different lines of business & channels of customers
- I = Illustration — Logo or overall look
- L = Location — How are you contacted? Address? Phone? Email? Website?

> **Authenticity** is what makes you verifiably trustable. What can you show your audience that you are trustworthy, authentic, and real? How can that be confirmed and verified?

RASCIL

RASCIL represent the **WHO** & **WHAT**. It is to be used as a general guide to help ensure facts aren't missed.

The origin of RASCIL is the design of yellow page ads

- R = Reliability — Length of service / longevity
- A = Authenticity — Certificates, licenses, degrees, accolades, testimonies
- S = Simplicity — Easy access to your product or service
- **C = Completeness — Different lines of business & channels of customers**
- I = Illustration — Logo or overall look
- L = Location — How are you contacted? Address? Phone? Email? Website?

Completeness is everything you are delivering to your audience. What is the list of deliverables are you presenting to your audience? Work on creating a bullet list and be complete.

15 ~ www.ForestAcademy.org ~ 15

Tying it all together. WIIFM & RASCIL combine with the 5 W's to make your marketing content

- WIIFM = (It/This) will (Make/Give) you __(why?/passion)__
- RASCIL = Reliability, Authenticity, Simplicity, Completeness, Illustration, Location
- 5 W's = Who, What, When, Where, Why

Together, they have a combined formula / Copyright (c) 2012, David K. Ewen, M.Ed.

Who

What ⊢ Who & What = RASCIL

When .... Time frame

Where .... Location

Why = WIIFM

Copyright (c) 2012, David K. Ewen, M.Ed.

Tying It All Together

This is the formula to represent yourself. It's easy to explain, but very hard to do.

- WIIFM = (It/This) will (Make/Give) you __(why?/passion)__
- RASCIL = Reliability, Authenticity, Simplicity, Completeness, Illustration, Location
- 5 W's = Who, What, When, Where, Why

Together, they have a combined formula / Copyright (c) 2012, David K. Ewen, M.Ed.

Who

What ⊢ Who & What = RASCIL

When .... Time frame

Where .... Location

Why = WIIFM

Copyright (c) 2012, David K. Ewen, M.Ed.

Example of Cardiologist writing a book about eating healthy

- WHO   Dr. David Ewen
- WHAT   Wrote a book about eating healthy
- WHEN   There will be a book signing next week
- WHERE   Signing at Barnes & Noble
- WHY   It will make you feel great

Same book, but described in another way

- WHO   Award winning cardiologist
- WHAT   The need to eat healthy
- WHEN   It's never too late
- WHERE   All across America
- WHY   This will give you good health

Remember

- WHEN is any type of Time Frame
- WHERE is any type of Location

といった # Writing The News Release

Purpose of News Release

Before writing a news release, it is important to first understand the purpose of a news release. The purpose is to receive and be interviewed and/or be represented in the media. To do that, a long winded news release is not necessary. In fact it is counterproductive and will prevent you from making contact with the media.

The media outlets do not have time to read lengthy news releases. They only need a tease to get them to reach you. Your incentive needs to be brief. A single paragraph completed with your name, affiliation, and direct cell phone number is all you need.

We studied the 5 W's and how it relates to the WIIFM formula and the RASCIL factors. On a piece of paper write the 5 W's: Who, What, When, Where, Why. List bullet items under each of the 5 W's listed. Finally mold the bullet items into a single paragraph of about 5 to 10 sentences. Focus on quality rather than quantity (ie, length). Spend the time on making an effective concise presentation rather than writing the complete lengthy article yourself. The media does not have time to read the detail-by-detail. That is their job. The news release is intended only to get the interview.

Writing a news release using the 5 W's along with WIIFM and RASCIL factors is not easy. It needs to be practiced and perfected over time. Make the effort to be effective in your presentation by taking the time to improve the quality of your news release and put less attention on the quantity (ie, length)

REMINDER: Difference Between Marketing & Publicity

The difference between marketing and publicity is the following:
- Marketing is what is said or written to the customer or client
- Publicity is the delivery of the marketing content.
- Sales is Marketing plus Publicity. Sales is Marketing planning first followed by Publicity.

21 ~ www.ForestAcademy.org ~ 21

Publicity

Traditional Newspapers
Broadcast Radio & TV
Online Web Outlets

Use All Of Your Resources

Your Local Broadcast Resources

You can take advantage of your local mainstream broadcast media. They all have websites with contact information.

(1) Email a news release using the 5 W's with RASCIL and WIIFM

(2) Print the email, and mail it

(3) Place your event on their website community calendar.

(4) Be available to answer the phone immediately

(5) Position your event near the TV or radio station so reporters don't have to travel.

(6) Do the same with newspapers.

23 ~ www.ForestAcademy.org ~ 23

Broadcast Radio

www.Radio-Locator.com

Search for radio shows by zip code.

Great opportunity to tour the country using the phone at home.

Local Network TV Affiliate

Search for Local TV stations

http://transition.fcc.gov/mb/engineering/dtvmaps

Search for your local network affiliate

NBC: http://www.nbc.com/local-stations
CBS: http://www.cbslocal.com/
ABC: http://site.abc.go.com/site/localstations.html
FOX: http://www.fox.com/affiliates.php

Get website of local stations to get contact info for sending your news release

25 ~ www.ForestAcademy.org ~ 25

Newspapers

Newspapers in the United States

http://www.OnlineNewspapers.com/USstate/USAtable.htm

Newspapers in the World

http://www.OnlineNewspapers.com

26 ~ www.ForestAcademy.org ~ 26

Magazines

Select Magazines by Genre or Category:

http://www.OnlineNewspapers.com/magazines

27 ~ www.ForestAcademy.org ~ 27

Internet Radio

The shows from internet radio are saved as podcasts. The links to saved shows can be shared on social media sites and email marketing. Find the best shows for you to reach out to.

The links of a previously aired online show can be shared on social media, email, blogs, and websites. They last "forever"

- www.BlogTalkRadio.com
- www.Live365.com/Genres/Talk
- www.VoiceAmerica.com/Home/Channels

Freelance Online Articles

An author can be nicely represented in a feature article. Send a news release out.

- www.Examiner.com
- www.AllVoices.com
- Voices.Yahoo.com
- www.HubPages.com
- Also, local newspapers

Share the feature article on social media (facebook, twitter, etc.)

Social Media

Take advantage of networking with your readers and fellow authors.

- www.Facebook.com
- www.Twitter.com
- LinkedIn.com

Share links from your feature articles and radio shows. Build a following.

Sending The News Release

Call-Write-Call

Check to see if the media resource has a phone number for reporting news. Usually local affiliate TV networks, local radio stations, and newspapers have a contact phone number. Ensure you have the right mailing address and email. The email most likely is a general email for reporting news.

1. Call and get name of news director, arts director, or event director
2. Verify the spelling of the name of your contact person.
3. Send by mail and email the news release
4. Ten days later, call back and confirm that news release arrived safely
5. You may have to make a few phone calls to ensure news release was read

Responding To Media Requests

Be Reachable

When a reporter or media specialist has your news release in hand, a call is made. If there is no answer, your news release is put to the side and another news release is acted upon. Not all news releases results in a story. By answering or not answering the phone can make the difference if your story gets the publicity it deserves.

The best option to be available is to have a cell phone on at all times with a bluetooth earpiece connected so that you have the ability to answer the phone right away and answer questions.

I remember a time when I was shopping, I received a call from a local TV affiliate reporter while she was driving her car. Because I answered, we were able to plan on having a satellite truck at an event for a LIVE on-the-air report in the morning news. The reporter told me that if I didn't answer when I did, then the local network would not have been at the event at all either LIVE or otherwise.

Be Convenient

Schedule your media event at a location near the TV station. TV reporters travel from one story to another and plan their day around the least amount of travel. This ensures enough stories are created and enough editing time is available to get all stories aired on time.

Radio stations typically have a morning broadcast during drive time for talking with guests. Be available for that early drive time so that you can be in the studio or on the phone.

Remember that any interview that is inconvenient for a reporter won't be done. Reporters work with a lot of stories. They will work the stories that give the least amount of resistance. You have to be accommodating to the media rather than the other way around.

Summary of Topics Completed

- Difference between marketing and publicity
- Marketing formula and strategy
- Publicity resources and media communication

Effective Publicity Using Media

David K. Ewen, M.Ed.

Forest Academy

37 ~ **www.ForestAcademy.org** ~ 37

www.ingramcontent.com/pod-product-compliance
Lightning Source LLC
Chambersburg PA
CBHW051225170526
45166CB00005B/2052